T0198856

Lord Why Am I Still In The Waiting Room!

Understanding the Importance on How and Why to Wait Well

TA-TANISHA THAMES

Order this book online at www.trafford.com
or email orders@trafford.com

Most Trafford titles are also available at major online book retailers.

Print information available on the last page.

ISBN: 978-1-4907-6038-4 (sc)
ISBN: 978-1-4907-6081-0 (e)

Library of Congress Control Number: 2015908108

Trafford rev. 05/22/2015

 www.trafford.com

North America & international
toll-free: 1 888 232 4444 (USA & Canada)
fax: 812 355 4082

Contents

Lord Why Am I Still In The Waiting Room!
Understanding the Importance on How and Why to Wait Well

Break Through Life Coach Ta-Tanisha Thames

Dedication

To my husband Darrick Thames, who always believed I could do it and made a sacrifice for me to do it, I love you more than you could ever know. To my mother Barbara Fisher who has always been there to pick up the pieces, I love you to the moon and back. To my sister La-Toya Dixon who had a dream of the reality coming forth I love you. To my prayer group who have always had my back, I appreciate you. Special thanks to LaTanya Evans, Latasha Guy, Patty Bunkley, Jessica & Leroy Redfield, David & Frenetta Green, Devon Lee, Stevie Biffle and Tammy Adkins for sowing in my life in so many ways, you will always be remembered and loved for that.

Introduction

"The Lord is good to those who wait for him, to the soul who seeks him"

Lamentations 3:25 NAS

I am one who doesn't like to wait for anything. I want things to happen quick, fast and in a hurry especially if I am in the equation. What a bad way to be when we are not in control over anything but God. I said I waited on God to make things happen in my life but then I had to take a step back to see if it was really me hurrying things along. We have to wait on a lot of things in life. To be noticed, to be married, to have kids, to get a job, to get a promotion, to buy a house or car, to move, to get over hurt or disappointment. It's always something and this could drive anybody crazy when you can't control your own destiny. Now I can understand why people are so angry and bitter with life. It doesn't make sense when they wanted what they wanted and God had another plan for them. It's very difficult living in this world if you say you are one of God's children and trying to make things happen when you want them to happen. Boy will your wait time seem forever. It reminds me when we have to go to the doctor because we know we need some help and answers about what we are going through. We have acknowledged we have something that is wrong with us and we need to seek the physician (God) to give us some answers on the matter. We go in confused, full of uneasiness, uncertainty and exhaustion. So many emotions that we should have given to God even before we entered in the waiting room. We go in with a premediated notion that we will be out in a hurry and our problem solved quickly. Boy, have we bamboozled ourselves into a trick bag. We are already agitated because of the many people we see waiting and the uncertainty if we will get the answers that we want to hear. Well I stop by to tell you that life is about waiting on God and his timing regardless if we agree with the process or not. We can resist, complain, murmur, have a temper tantrum and shut the world out, it doesn't make a difference when God is at work in your life. We long to hear God and feel his presence but when this is not taking place quickly we drift further and further from Him. This very thing makes us impatient and causes us to abandon the very thing God has us waiting on. We have made ourselves believe that our answers are better than Gods. What a way to think when God knows the end of a thing than its beginning. "I make know the end from the beginning, from ancient times, what is still to come. I say my purpose will stand and I will do all that I please." (Isaiah 46:10 NIV). So why are we at war in the waiting room? Why do we constantly go back and forth with God on his plan and timing for our lives? He will prevail every time. "Many are the plans in a man's heart, but it is the Lord's purpose that prevails." (Proverbs 19:21 NIV). Thank God that God knows us individually inside and out. He knows it's hard for us to abandon control, and to trust fully in Him. But God always have a plan even in our stubbornness.

I believe learning to turn over our will for his will, will be the greatest challenge that we will ever face. Learning how to let go and let God should be one of the first things we relinquish entering into the waiting room. No one said it would be easy but it can be done through trusting God and believing in the promises that He has spoken for our lives. "For I know the plans I have for you, declares the Lord, plans to prosper you and not to harm you, plans to give you hope and a future." (Jeremiah29:11 NIV). If we just trust Him there is so much He wants us to see and learn while waiting on Him. This maybe the very reason why we are still in the waiting room and so frequently. Let us learn what we need to learn while waiting. Let us not get caught up in the web on how quickly He answers us or somebody else. Let us not ignore when God is working in our lives even in the quiet and non-movement times. Let us not try to hurry along the process or we may miss what God is trying to do and say. "Be still, and know that I am God: I will be exalted among the nations, I will be exalted in the earth." (Psalm 46:10). Know that it won't be a quick but learn how to wait well by following God's word, remembering his promise and surrendering your will over. By doing these things it will draw you further away from your problem and closer to God and what he wants for your life. Everything is based on a choice to do something. Chose to wait well on God no matter what the cost or how long it takes. The surprising thing is after God finishes working on us, taking out somethings and putting in somethings we will realize it was worth the wait regardless if we get what we were waiting for or not. Let's not be afraid to wait because the reward in the end is worth waiting for.

Waiting Room

Chapter 1

How Did I Get To the Waiting Room?

"I, Daniel, was troubled in spirit, and the visions
that passed through my mind disturbed me."
Daniel 7:15 NIV

Like, Daniel I was troubled in my heart and spirit and what I was thinking and what I saw all around me disturbed me. I was losing rest and peace and this was not what God promised me. If you are stubborn like me at times listen up, I have some news for you. Acknowledge that something is wrong and quickly run to the waiting room to get your diagnosis. Don't leave, no matter how long it may take because this very diagnosis may save your life.

I'm going to be as honest with you as I can because the lessons I learned taught me how to surrender and to wait well. I knew there was something wrong in my life but I just couldn't put my finger on it. How could this be that things are not happening for me as fast as they use to. I've had to wait for somethings but not as long as I have been waiting in this particular season in my life. I would tell myself God wouldn't do this to me. I knew what I was waiting for would be here tomorrow and when tomorrow came and it didn't happen I would grant God some grace and extend Him another day. Really, who am I to dictate to God on when the timing is right. I did read where he said, "He said to them: "It is not for you

to know the times or dates the Father has set by his own authority".
(Acts 1:7 NIV). So whatever I was going through it was a part of
God's timing and planning.

I guess you maybe wandering how did I get to the waiting room.
Let me give you an illustration by using an analogy. You know
how you notice all the symptoms of when a cold is coming on.
You begin to get a sore throat, runny nose, congestion, coughing
or even a fever. You try to do everything possible to get rid of it but
nothing is working. You are irritable and cranky so now you decide
to see a physician. You need a diagnosis and a prescription quickly
to get you healed. What we have failed to realized is that colds are
caused by viruses and antibiotics do not help fight viruses. They
may do more harm than good. They may ease your discomfort
but when having a viral infection it has to run its course. So it's
not on your timing but its own timing. You have waited to be
told you have to wait for it to run its course. Now what do you
do? Listen to the doctor and be still and let it run its course. So it
is when we are wanting answers in our personal lives. We can see
all the symptoms. Waiting on a job for several months that now
has turned into years. Waiting for someone to love us and all signs
point towards they don't or won't. Your money have been depleted
and there is no other sources coming in to replenish it. The kids are
acting out and you can't seem to find a resolution anywhere. Your
marriage is all messed up and you don't see a light at the end of
the tunnel and to top it all off your friends have scattered and you
see the road does not link back to you. I could go on and on but
you know your symptoms better than I do. Just like the cold we
notice all the symptoms to our problems and it's weighing us down.
Any actions that we're taking to resolve the problem isn't working.
We've tried it all. Now we are irritable, cranky and tired.

So what do we do, or should do. First, acknowledge that you do see
the symptoms. Second, acknowledge that you can't find a remedy
within yourself. Third and lastly run to the waiting room to meet
the physician (God) so He can fix it. He can tell you the diagnosis

and give you a prescription. Just remember it's on his timing not yours. You never know when the doctor may pop in.

I can tell you from experience that I'm always in the waiting room and I have learned it's a good thing. Just as fast as I get there I am back there again for something else. Know that it wasn't that easy for me and it took me awhile to get to this point. I was stubborn, selfish, spoiled and not submissive. I wanted what I wanted when I wanted it and if you were to slow at getting it for me I would get it myself. Sounds like an impatient person to me. Impatience is what I was and finally God got a hold of me. I could no longer ask other people to solve my problems or solve it myself and neither could I work my way out of it. This one problem that I could not seem to solve pushed me into the waiting room and boy did I go in kicking and screaming.

Life was good to me. I had any and everything a girl could ever ask for. A good husband, a great family, a good job, good friends and any want I desired. Well the ship came to bay when my company decided to close the doors at my site I was located in. No worries for me I thought. I had options. I was offered a relocation package to Arizona but declined for many reasons. I had a big bonus coming so I knew I could go without working for about a year and I was collecting unemployment. I was enjoying life as if I were still working. Shopping, eating, traveling and every want and need still being met. My year had passed and I was ready to get back in the work field. Unemployment stopped after six months and when I tried to file again they denied my claim due to a period of not working in the months I was claiming. Really, what about all the other years I worked. But no worries, I wasn't going to cry over spilled milk, my husband was still holding down the fort. But I was ready to go back to work. I missed people and physically dressing up going into a building and having contact with people. So my search began for a new job. Application after application. Denial after denial. What was the problem, I sure had the credentials on what I was applying for. Every door seemed to be shut even in other locations. Well one year of waiting has turned into almost 1 year and a half. Surely the Lord knows I want a job. What was taking Him so long to grant my request? I wasn't asking for much. I then began to see my husband robbing Peter to pay Paul and trying to keep his head above water. At one point he even said go find a part time job. I desperately wanted to help him.

I was struggling with personal cravings that needed to be satisfied as well, I liked to shop. I saw my symptoms and tried every remedy I thought would work to cure my problems but they were not working. Then the war began to take place in my head. It started messing with my self-esteem and I began to go on a downward spiral. I had my good days and I had my bad days with self-pity being my friend. I figured this was a personal matter so no one else didn't need to know my inward struggles even though I showed the symptoms on the outside. I was tired and weak and needed to get to the physician (God) before things got worse with me. You see I was trying to eliminate the symptoms before they elevated themselves. I realized I was doing it all wrong and because of that it caused me to run as fast as I could to get to the waiting room. Nothing else mattered except seeing God the physician and getting some answers. This is when I decided to enter the waiting room.

Chapter 2

How Long is the Wait Time?

"So be patient, Brethren (as you wait) til the coming of the Lord. See how the farmer waits expectantly for the precious harvest from the land. (See how) he keeps up his patient (vigil) over it until it receives the early and late rains. So you also must be patient. Establish your hearts (strengthen and confirm them in the final certainty, for the coming of the Lord is very near.)"

James 5:7-8 Amplified

I have arrived at the waiting room not knowing what to expect but at least I've made it. I'm taken back to the illustration where the patient who had symptoms of a cold has arrived in the waiting room and waiting to see the intake nurse. The first thing they notice is the clock on the wall and it becomes their enemy. Even though they have not been their long impatience begins to settle in and before you know it there're upset with everybody even the clock.

So it is with me and many of you. We have finally made it to the waiting room and we have the nerves to be impatience and in a rush to be seen. God is probably thinking it took you long enough to get here. Relax for a while and wait on your turn to been seen.

What we fail to remember is that even before we see the physician (God) we have to wait to been seen by the intake nurse (Holy Spirit) as well.

> "In the same way, the spirit helps us in our weakness. We do not know what we ought to pray for, but the spirit himself intercedes for us with groans that words cannot express.
>
> Romans 8:26 NIV

Right now my emotions are all over the place and I am clearly not thinking right. In these times I need the help of the Holy Spirit or shall I say the intake nurse. I know that the intake nurse (Holy Spirit) will help bring things into perspective for me. I know their primary goal is to listen, comfort and guide me. I have confidence knowing the intake nurse (Holy Spirit) will not steer me in the wrong direction, I have done a great job of doing that myself. So I tell myself and suggest you do the same to surrender and just wait on Him.

As I sit here in the waiting room my mind finally cease from being bombarded with many thoughts and a peace comes over me. I then can clearly hear the Intake Nurse (Holy Spirit) saying come. You see if the enemy can keep you worked up in your emotions he knows you will never get to the place of peace where you can hear that small quiet voice saying to come.

"But when he, the spirit of truth comes, he will guide you into all truth. He will not speak of his own; he will speak only what he hears, and he will tell you what is yet to come." John 16:13 NIV

I thought what a joy to tell somebody else your problems. I can let it all out on the table. I will not withhold anything. This is my moment where I can let the intake nurse (Holy Spirit) know every symptom I am having so he can give the physician an accurate account of what's going on with me. This is where true repentance starts. No holding back for me.

It is such a great relief when you can talk about what's affecting you even though an answer has not been given to you as of yet. I felt at ease knowing the intake nurse (Holy Spirit) was writing it all down to give a correct account to the Physician.

As I waited I became so observant on what was going on around me. It can drive you insane if you don't stay focused on why you are there. I'm waiting patiently and notice that seconds have turned into minutes and minutes have turned into hours. This peace that I once had was gone. I stare at a door that is being opened and closed as people go in and out. I'm wondering when it's going to be my turn. I'm beginning to feel uneasy and antsy and would like these feeling to diminish quickly so I begin to think about scriptures to help me. I remembered the one that said, "Wait on the Lord, be of good courage, and he shall strengthen thine heart, wait, I say, on the Lord."

Psalm: 27:14 KJV

Right now I needed strengthening in thine heart because I felt like my heart was hardening. I needed some answers now and this waiting wasn't helping me at all. The more time past, the more anxious and irritable I became. I had to dig deep to find another scripture to help me get through this. I ponder on the scripture, "But they that wait upon the Lord shall renew their strength; they shall mount up with wings as eagles; they shall run, and not be weary; and they shall walk, and not faint." Isaiah 40:31 KJB

I begin to ask God was I being tested even in the waiting room. I wanted the promise of waiting well but I felt as though I was failing miserably. I wanted my wings but I was weary and felt as though I was fainting. I wasn't doing well at this point and began to flip the script. Why me Lord. I tried to plead my case by telling God how wonderful I was and how I had done such great things for Him. All I could hear myself say is why, me Lord. I was a mess. I now have an attitude and I find the intake nurse and ask how much longer do I have to wait. It's been hours. In a small quiet voice I hear the words, "For the vision is yet for an appointed time, but at the end it shall speak, and not lie; though it tarry, wait for it; because it will surely come, it will not tarry." Habkkuk 2:3 KJV

In plan terms, be patient! I will work out my plans in my perfect timing not yours. I realized at that moment I wasn't doing a great job of just waiting and I saw how impatient I really was. I felt so embarrassed after being chastised. I quietly begin to ask God to teach me how to wait well even when I don't understand the process. I took my seat and begin to close my eyes and just meditate on what I should do now.

Chapter 3

What Should I do in the Waiting Room

So the Lord must wait for you to come to him so he can show you his love and compassion. For the Lord is a faithful God. Blessed are all those who wait for him." Isaiah 30:18 NLT

As I began to meditate, I asked myself what should I be doing while waiting in the waiting room. If I am going to wait I might as well make it productive and make it count for something. As I sit blocking out everything that is around me, I begin to remember some of the things the intake nurse (Holy Spirit) had shared with me. Three things were brought back to my remembrance.

Number one: You have to let go and let God do His part.

> "Come to me all you who are weary and burdened, and I will give you rest. Take my yoke upon you and learn from me, for I am gentle and humble in heart, and you will find rest for your souls." Matthew 11:28-30

I knew I was carrying around a heavy load that was weighing me down both mentally and physically. I was finally sick of being sick of being tired. God stated to come if you were weary and burdened and I was both. He promised rest and that's exactly what

I needed but before I could get the rest that he promised I had to be honest with what was burdening me. This was my first Aha moment! You can't conquer what you can't let go of. I realized my biggest problem was me. I was standing in my own way of getting what I needed. I had to take ownership that everything that was happening to me I had some kind of involvement in the matter. If I said I trusted God with everything that concerns me, why was I allowing self to get in the way of that. I knew if I wanted to be free of any sickness that I had been carrying around I would have to go back down a dark road to let go of somethings that were attached to me. I was up to the challenge, I had to wait anyway.

It's never easy of letting go of things that make us feel secure or safe regardless if they are healthy for us or not. We tend to cling on to things that will make our emotions feel good even though it may be only temporal. Nobody ever said life would be easy but when that curve ball hits you in the head and you now have a concussion, it all becomes a blur. You've been hurt, disappointed, rejected and scared by what life has thrown at you and now you're ducking at everything.

I have learned it's difficult to go through life with being weighed down with what you can't conquer or forgive. I was tired of playing a game that I was being cheated at every time. You stole my joy, peace and love and I wanted it all back. I learned by getting back those things I had to give up somethings. I had to give up worry, unforgiveness and pride. I was ready to let go of the things that were affecting me both physically in my body and mentally in my mind. I wanted to be free so I could get all that God had for me. I wanted to be empty of the junk so God could pour in his healing oil.

As I began to look back over my life things began to surface which I have had hidden for so long. I started thinking about people, circumstances and situations that I had not let go of. I heard God say open your mouth and let them go. So I opened my mouth and said, I release you and forgive you _____, I'm moving on. No longer will you take up residency here. I evict you now in the name of Jesus! Rejection, fear of the unknown, not being accepted or loved you will go back to the sender who sent you. No more holding on to my own will. I wanted what God had for me and instantly I felt much lighter and at peace.

I wanted to be free and it's only through surrounding and letting go and letting God do his part. "Cast your cares on the Lord and he will sustain you; he will never let the righteous fall." Psalm 55:22 NKJ

What a great promise to us. Now it's your turn what are you willing to let go of so you can be healed.

The second thing that came back to my remembrance was to be patience. "I waited patiently for the Lord; he turned to me and heard my cry." Psalm 44:1 NIV

I had learned to let go and now I had to be patience for God to continue to do his work. I realized many things had been passed down the years to me illegally and I needed God to eradicate them. I knew this would take some time but I was ready. I needed God to mend some cracks that were in my soul. I knew it wouldn't be an overnight process but I was standing on promise that God heard my cry and He would answer. I just had to keep in mind that it would be in his timing not mines. My goal was to suppress restlessness and allow the peace of God to surpass me. The funny thing is that I thought letting go was the easy part but found out it was more difficult just to be patience. "But let patience have her perfect work, that ye may be perfect and entire, wanting nothing." James 1:4 KJV

I needed patience to have its perfect work in me. I was willing to be put on the potter's wheel, where God could shape and mold me into what He wanted me to become.

Are you patience enough for God to shape you?

The third and last thing I remember the intake nurse (Holy Spirit) saying was, while you wait listen to the instructions on what God's will is for your life.

> "For I know the plans I have for you, declares the Lord, plans to prosper you and not to harm you, plans to give you hope and a future."
> Jeremiah 29;11 NIV

Had I been so selfish that I had not noticed if I was doing God's will or not. Was I so pre-occupied with what I wanted for my life that I had missed out on the plans that God had for me. I thought back to all the other times I was seeking direction and I felt like I did get instructions. What was so different about this time? Why was I so unsure of the plans that God had for me. Were we not on the same page? Had my plans for the way I wanted my life to go superseded Gods?

I then recall on how God has been dealing with me over this last past year and a half. I realized I hadn't sought God on a continuance basis until I lost my job. Was he trying to get my attention? Did he have another plan? I needed to know because things were way out of alignment.

My prayer was Lord as I wait on you, give me ears to hear only you, eyes to show me what you want and a heart to receive it. I was not going to allow self or the enemy to get in the way of what God had in store for me. I made a conscious decision that I was going to seek God out until I found Him to get my instructions. "You will seek me and find me, when you seek me with all your heart."

Jeremiah 29:13 ESV

I was thirsty and I knew only God could quench this kind of thirst. I remember the intake nurse (Holy Spirit) saying that I had to remove all road blocks getting in the way of me hearing from God. I had to remove myself from all the noise and get in a quiet place to meet Him. I had to be willing to deny myself so I could find myself. I was on a mission. "As the deer pants for streams of water, so my soul pants for you, O God."

Psalm 42:1-2 NIV

I learned you have to be persistent when seeking God. It's on a continuance basis, not just when you need something. I learned that He also needs something from us. We are the ones that are still left here on earth. I had to be in attendance to get the instructions on what was needed to be done here on earth. I finally got it and the interaction from that point between God and myself was phenomenal. I would talk and write to God in my daily designated time and He would reciprocate by answering through his word, dreams and visions, prophecy or by speaking through circumstances and situations. It took discipline and dedication but it was worth it.

I had to block out what everybody and self was saying and focus on what God was saying. I had to learn to throw out all the misconceptions about what I should be doing in the waiting room and just trust God on what He wanted me to do.

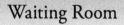

Waiting Room

Chapter 4

Misconceptions about
the Waiting Room

> "Meaningless! Meaningless! Says the teacher.
> Utterly meaningless! Everything is meaningless."
> Ecclesiastes 1:2 NIV

If I had listen to all the wonderful people who gave me advice about my symptoms, I don't think I would have ever entered into the waiting room. People can only give you what they have and if you listen well you will surely find out what they have in them. For the heart speaks volumes. "For whatever is in your heart determines what you say. A good person produces good things from the treasury of a good heart, and an evil person produces evil things from the treasury of an evil heart." Matthew 12:34-35

Now don't get me wrong all the advice that was given was not bad. But for those who allowed their waiting room experience to overtake them, only unpleasant advice manifested. So unpleasant that it would make you think twice about even entering into the waiting room. By trial and error I had to learn to throw out the bones and only eat the meat. I realized that we were all made differently and everyone has their own opinion. What makes you so unique is how you deal with trails and tribulations. Depending on

- 14 -

how that trial and tribulation worked on us and in us determines what is going to come out of us. It either makes you into a stronger individual or it breaks you to becoming a weak individual. So don't be surprised by what comes out of man's mouth and how they interact. We are only to concentrate on how it will cause an effect on our lives.

I know that storms will come but it is only to show us what our true foundation is made of. "For any building, the foundation is critical. It must be deep and solid enough to withstand any storms that may come our way. The quality of your foundation will determine the quality of how you stand. Too often we use defaulted or warped material and when test or storms come, we begin to crumble. This causes a derogatory effect on our behavior which will soon appear in what we say and do.

It reminds me of the story Job and I just want to focus on his three so called friends who came to silently grieve with him. Job was agonizing over his situation which I will call (the waiting room). His three friends came to sympathize and comfort him but to later find out their words of comfort were not helpful but destructive. They were misleading by their own insensitive advice. They blamed his suffering or symptoms on some sin he must have committed. Did they go through something in their own waiting room experience that is now causing them to put their judgments on Job? Be careful of those who you allow to share your waiting room experience with. They are eager to voice their opinion on what they believe to be right about your situation. Job friends were dead wrong about Job and so could be your friends.

Many will come and give us advice and comforting during our waiting room experience but BEWARE of what comes out of their mouth. Once it comes out of the mouth and entertained you can't give it back. Everybody's experience is not alike and what make them weak may make you strong or vice a versa. Job friends couldn't convince him and neither should yours if it is not lining up with the word of God and what God has promised you. Remember in the end God eventually spoke to Job and his waiting room experience ended with him being restored to happiness and wealth. This is what we want our outcome of waiting in the waiting room to look like. God speaking to us. This is the whole reason we are in the waiting room in the first place. It is easy to rely on others for the answers but in reality, only God knows exactly why things happen as they do.

Listed below you will find some of the misconceptions about the waiting room experience.

Misconception Number 1: It's meaningless, you could be waiting for years for what you have desired and still see it not come to pass.

Correction: Psalm 37:4 NIV

> "Take delight in the Lord, and he will give you the desires of your heart."

Misconception Number 2: Sitting and waiting can cause you to lose hope when you don't see it manifest as quickly as it should.

Correction: Romans 8:25 NLT

> "But if we look forward to something we don't yet have, we must wait patiently and confidently."

Misconception Number 3: Waiting can draw you further away from the promise when see everyone else being answered and not you.

Correction: Psalm 37:7 NIV

"Be still before the Lord and wait patiently for him; do not fret when people succeed in their way, when they carry out their wicked schemes."

Misconception Number 4: It seems as if there is always something happening that is taking you backwards while being in the waiting room.

Correction: Philippians 4:11-13 NIV

"I am not saying this because I am in need, for I have learned to be content whatever the circumstances. I know what it is to be in need, and I know what it is to have plenty. I have learned the secret of being content in any and every situation, whether well fed or hungry, whether living in plenty or in want. I can do everything through him who gives me strength."

Misconception Number 5: No matter how long you wait and deny yourself of what you want, it seems in the end, you still have lost.

Correction: 1 Peter 1:6-7 NIV

"In all this you greatly rejoice, though now for a little while you may have had to suffer grief in all kinds of trials. These have come so that the proven genuineness of your faith-of greater worth than gold, which perishes even though refined by fire-may result in praise, glory and honor when Jesus Christ is revealed."

Misconceptions by people will come but know that God has a correction to turn it around. It is your mind set and how you perceive it that will get you through. If you can apply the lesson of when life gives you lemons, make some lemonade you will be able to counteract any misconceptions about the waiting room experience. I will leave you with 2 Corinthians 10:5 ESV says, "We destroy arguments and every lofty opinion raised against the knowledge of God, and take every thought captive to obey Christ." Taking those misconceptions and holding them captive does nothing for you. It's only when they are not entertained that will cause you to wait well.

Chapter 5

Who else is in the Waiting Room

"Come to me, all you who are weary and burdened,
and I will give you rest." Matthew 11:28 NIV

As I looked around the waiting room it seemed to be more people waiting from when I first entered. People were scattered everywhere. From sitting in chairs to standing. They all had a place of waiting. I noticed every race could be account for and gender both young and old. No one was exempt from the waiting room experience. During this time I was much more attentive than before and I could sense all the emotions that were flying around in the air. You know anyone can change the atmosphere of a place. The expressions on their faces and how they behaved told off on them. Some looked happy to be there while others looked unhappy. Some looked frustrated while others looked as if they were at peace. As I surveyed the room I could hear people sharing stories on how and what got them to the waiting room. I was still waiting so I thought I would indulge in their matters. I thought maybe their story would be more intriguing than mine.

I could hear the man in the back of me shouting as loud as he could as he shared his story with the person sitting next to him. As I listened I summed his story up to be tragic. His question was, what does pleasure really accomplishes.

Ecclesiastes 2:10-11 NIV

> "I denied myself nothing my eyes desired; I refused
> my heart no pleasure. My heart took delight in all
> my labor, and this was the reward for all my toil.
> Yet when I surveyed all that my hands had done
> and what I had toiled to achieve, everything was
> meaningless, a chasing after the wind; nothing was
> gained under the sun."

You see this man was seeking to find life's meaning but to only realize it was as chasing after the wind. He could feel it as it passes but he couldn't catch hold of it. In all his accomplishments even the ones he bragged about the most, he now realizes it was on temporary. It pleased him for just a moment. He thought security and his self-worth were tied in these accomplishments. He is now so burdened with disappointment that he needs some answers to get him back on track.

What I got from his story was, be careful where you place your time, energy and money.

I looked across from me and I saw this lady standing. She was pacing back and forth as she talked to herself. I thought this was very strange since she was in a room full of people. But I assumed something drastic must have happened to drive her to this point. As I watched her pace back and forth I could hear her questioning God saying,

Ecclesiastes 2:18-20

> "I hated all the things that I had toiled for under
> the sun, because I must leave them to the one who
> comes after me. And who knows whether that
> person will be wise or foolish? Yet they will have
> control over all the fruit of my toil into which I

have poured my effort and skill under the sun. This too is meaningless. So my heart began to despair over all my toilsome labor under the sun."

You see this woman was dying from some disease and all she was concerned about was where her money would be going. She was finally realizing that all her hard work bears no fruit for those who work solely to earn money and gain possessions. She realizes now that she should have been doing something wisely with it but now it will be left to someone who didn't earn it.

What I gained from her story was. be careful on what you do with your money because what is gained may be lost if you're not putting it to good use.

As I looked to my left, I saw this middle class woman sitting next to me with her hands covering her face. She was singing a song filled with much melody and joy. I thought to myself she must be at peace while she is waiting. She kept singing the same thing over and over and it went like this.

Psalm 23 NIV

> The Lord is my shepherd, I lack nothing. He makes me lie down in green pastures, he leads me besides quiet waters, and he refreshes my soul. He guides me along the right paths for his name's sake. Even though I walk through the darkest valley, I will fear no evil, for you are with me; your rod and your staff, they comfort me. You prepare a table before me in the presence of my enemies. You anoint my head with oil; my cup overflows. Surely your goodness and love will follow me all the days of my life, and I will dwell in the house of the Lord forever."

After listening over and over again to her song I realized she wasn't questioning God on why she was there but thanking him. She trusted Him as her Shepherd to lead, guide and protect her while she was going through her waiting room experience. What I got from her was that she was content. By her allowing God to help and guide her through this waiting room process she was at peace. She had something more valuable than any of them had while being there. She knew that God knew the "green pastures" and quiet waters in her life and that he would restore her. I could tell this woman had been here before because she knew how to submit without fighting it. She had put down her will and had picked up God's will on what he wanted for her. It seemed at this point nothing else really mattered. Just watching her took me to another place in learning how to wait well on God.

I learned that there will be all types of people in the waiting room and if you listen well you may learn a thing or two. Everybody story is different and everybody has their own way of dealing with their own sickness. This is not a time to judge but be thankful for your own symptoms. The point we need to grab a hold of is, they made it to the waiting room and hopefully nothing will distract them from getting what they need.

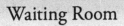

Chapter 6

Beware of Distractions in the Waiting Room

"Stay alert! Watch out for your great enemy, the devil. He prowls around like a roaring lion, looking for someone to devour. 1 Peter 5:8 NIV

What I have learned while waiting in the waiting room is you can easily get distracted when your faith starts to waiver. It's one thing to wait but when waiting for long periods of time and not seeing the promise around it can cause you to venture off in to things that mean you know good. It looks good, smell good but not good for you.

The enemy knows that if you wait and wait well there is a reward for you in the end. His primary goal is for you not to obtain it. He will use whoever and whatever to lure you out of the waiting room. He is slick and will use situations and people to help him snare his target. Many people have left the waiting room for this very reason. They got distracted by what they see and hear instead of holding on the promise of why they were there in the first place. I had to learn that the enemy was cunning and if you entertain him in the least bit, he has an open door to come in and cause havoc.

I am going to share with you some of the distractions that I struggled with while being in the waiting room. Hopefully by sharing these distractions you will be able to relate and instantly know how to go the other way.

My number one distraction was people. At first I thought I was being tortured over and over again but to only realize God was working somethings in me and somethings out of me. The enemy thought he could use people to get me distracted but God was even working in that. I learned while waiting it's easy to get distracted by focusing on other people when nothing is happening for you. I noticed the very things I longed for people I knew personally were being blessed with. Doors were being opened up for them that I felt like should be opening up for me as well. I didn't want the feeling of jealousy to have its way because I knew this would be a tactic of the enemy. I was happy for my friends and family that doors of new opportunities were opening but I couldn't help to think about when it would be my turn. It was an honest feeling I was feeling and I decided to explore with it. Bad mistake but it only lead me down a woe is me party. I knew better than that. I didn't know how long they had been waiting in the waiting room for their remedy. This was a time to rejoice with them instead of focusing on self. Self will always lead you down a path of destruction so I got excited for them and reminded myself, "For God does not show favoritism." Romans 2:11 NIV. What He does for one, He can do the same thing with another. I just needed to wait my turn. This distraction using people could have turned out differently if the enemy had its way but I was on top of it. The enemy wanted me to get depressed and even mad at those who were getting their remedy. He wanted me to focus on how they were getting theirs and me not getting mine. He wanted me to question God on when and if He was going to do it for me. I couldn't get caught up in that type of drama. It takes to much energy and useless time. It works on your heart to harden it and it will draw you further from God. I had come too far to walk out of the waiting room on something that was so trivial. I knew the enemy just wanted to blow things out of proportion.

Take note that in the waiting room, "Do not be anxious about anything, but in everything situation, by prayer and petition, with thanksgiving, present your requests to God. And the peace of God, which transcends all understanding, will guard your hearts and your minds in Christ Jesus." Philippians 4:6-7 NIV

The enemy will use the very thing that you are anxious about and will taunt you with it. He's so dirty that he will use the closet things around you.

The second distraction the enemy tried to use was situations. Sitting in the waiting room you would think your only focus would be on you and you getting the help you need. But why all of a sudden you feel like you're dealing with everybody else's situations. They got themselves into the situation and now they needed your help to get them out of it. This was not my problem and I was feeling heavy about somebody else's problem. I was caring burdens that were not meant for me to carry. I was feeling stressed out and over whelmed. At times I wanted to say, Lord I can't wait any longer the stresses of dealing with others situations has caused me to want to get out of here. I knew this was what the enemy wanted. I reminded myself of the story of Mary and Martha and how they opened up their home to Jesus and his disciples. Mary sat at the Lord's feet listening to what he said while Martha was distracted by all the preparations that had to be made. Martha was upset about her sister not helping and wanted Jesus to tell her to help her. "Martha, Martha", the Lord answered, "you are worried and upset about many things, but only one thing is needed, Mary has chosen what is better, and it will not be taken away from her." Luke 10:41-42 ISV

Reflecting on this made me look at my own dilemma I was dealing with. I didn't want to get so busy occupied with other people situations that I missed out on what I was waiting for. Time to be with the Physician. Learning to say no was ok, it was a choice and I was learning to set the right priorities. The enemy wanted me to engage myself into other people's situations which was only busy work. His goal was to take my attention off of the Physician.

Take note that in the waiting room you have to, "set your mind on things that are above, not on things that are on earth." Colossians 3:2 KJV. They will distract you every time.

The third distraction the enemy tried to use against me was my mind. My mind was racing with what I had and what I didn't have. Focusing on the seen and laboring with the unseen. I was driving myself crazy. I asked God to, "Search me, O God, and know my heart. Test me and know my anxious thoughts. Point out anything in me that offends you, and lead me along the path of everlasting life." Psalm 139:23-24 NIV

I wanted to be on a path of everlasting life but I was limiting myself getting there by allowing the enemy to distort my mind. I know off hand the mind is one way the enemy can torment you. If he can get to the mind he can formulate a distorted thought, the thought begins to manifest out of the mouth and now it has entered the heart. By not taking captive of this fraudulent thought it will rule you instead of you ruling it. I know what the scripture said about, "Casting down imaginations, and every high thing that exalteth itself against the knowledge of God, and bringing into captivity every though to the obedience of Christ." 2 Corinthians 10:5

I tried several times but it seemed as if the enemy was winning this battle. How could he be winning if God said the battle against me had already been won? Did I really believe this? Somehow I had allowed the enemy to paint doubt and unbelief with just a thought and I needed to take back my peace of mind. I was in a battle and I was ready to fight. I remembered the scripture, "Peace I leave with you, my peace I give to you. Not as the world gives do I give to you. Let not your heart be troubled, neither let it be afraid." John 14:27 ESV

I had to cast fear out of my life if I was going to recapture my peace. I needed to take back what the enemy was stealing from me. I knew the greatest weapon I had to combat that tormenting enemy was repeating God's word back to him. When he spoke, I had to quickly respond before allowing the thought to consume me. Trust me it's a losing battle if you don't have any word in you. This is where the enemy has gained so much ground and has held many of us captive. He keeps us so distracted and preoccupied with unnecessary concerns that we don't have time to get ready for the battle. His mission is to get us worn out even before the battle has started. Don't get caught off guard, know your weapons to use for the brawl. I had to make myself find the ammunition that was needed for my daily mind struggles.

When he said: I was weak and I wasn't going to make it.

I found my ammunition by telling him: "That's why I take pleasure in my weakness, and in the insults, hardships, persecutions, and troubles that I suffer for Christ. For when I am weak, then I am strong." 2 Corinthians 12:10 NLT

When he said: Look God is not taking care of your needs.

I found my ammunition by telling him: "And my God will supply every need of yours according to his riches in glory in Christ Jesus." Philippians 4:19 ESV. He said, "Consider the ravens; they neither sow nor reap, they have neither store house nor barn, and yet God feeds them. Of how much more value are you than the birds." Luke 12:24 ESV

When he said: You will never find rest for your soul.

I found my ammunition by telling him: "Take my yoke upon you, and learn from me, for I am gentle and lowly in heart, and you will find rest for your souls. For my yoke is easy, and my burden is light." Matthew 11:29-30 ESV

When he said: You will always fall into temptation.

I found my ammunition by telling him: "No temptation has overtaken you that is not common to man. God is faithful, and he will not let you be tempted beyond your ability, but with the temptation he will also provide the way of escape, that you may be able to endure it." 1 Corinthians 10:13 ESV

The secret is out on how to win the battle against the enemy when he is at work. Know the way the enemy tries to work on our minds will all differ. He will use where you are at spiritually and where your carnal state of mind is and devise his plan of action. Be proactive and have something in your arsenal to take action with. You can only give out what you have in you so suit up for the battle with the word fighting for you. It's useless when trying to do it on your own. It's a slow death both spiritually and physically.

Waiting Room

Chapter 7

The Reward on Waiting Well

"Let's not get tired of doing what is good. T just
the right time we will reap a harvest of blessing if
we don't give up." Galatians 6:9 NLT

As I sit in the waiting room waiting on the Physician (God). I
realize this is my final conclusion on the matter of "Lord why am
I still in the Waiting Room." I'm at the part where I am supposed
to be telling you about the reward in waiting well. Unfortunately,
I won't be able to tell you about the reward I received because I
yet to have received it. But don't get disappointed for me because
what I did receive is far more precious and valuable than the reward
itself. I must admit that I was a little disappointed because I wanted
to end this book by telling you what a great reward I received in
the end for waiting so well but God had another plan. He quickly
reminded me, you know what I have promised you. "God is not a
man, so he does not lie. He is not human, so he does not change his
mind. Has he ever spoken and failed to act? Has he ever promised
and not carried it through?" Numbers 23:19 NLT So what are you
worried about it will come, just keep trusting me. I asked God, is
this what I am to tell the people to just keep waiting and doing
good and the reward will eventually come. I heard Him say no,
share with the people on the real reward on waiting well. You see,
the real reward is not getting the promise because you know that

is a given. The real reward on waiting well is the chasing after God to receive it. Wow, this was the Aha moment that we all have been looking for. God said it was the pursuit of chasing me and not quitting whether you received the reward or not. By chasing me along the way you realized I was much more important than the reward itself.

I had been in this waiting room for a while and I went through a lot to get there and to stay there. My symptoms is what drove me there but my determination is what kept me there. I was determined to see the Physician at any cost. Nothing is worth waiting for if it doesn't cost you something. It cost me my job but it was worth it. The longer I stayed in the waiting room the more naked I became at stripping away those things that were not like God. I was on the potter's wheel and He was shaping and molding me into what He wanted me to become. I had to get myself prepared and ready for my reward. I realized that every day I waited my reward seemed less important. I had finally got a clue that in order to get the reward I had to fill that space of waiting by finding the rewarder Himself.

There were times where I filled it with sorrow, unbelief and hopelessness to only realize this was only prolonging the process and me getting my reward. I knew I had to do something different in order to get something different. So I traded in my symptoms for a cure. I learned that I had to take each day one day at a time, getting all that I needed in that day. Not being concerned about tomorrow because tomorrow had its own challenges. I only had my today and I only wanted what God had for me. Every day He was changing my desires. He was taking things out that meant me no good and adding things in to edify, encourage and build me up. Every day I was making a sacrifice not my will to be done but the Physician (God) will to be done.

I knew asking for God's will would put me in a position that my reward could go either way. But I was so fixed at being at peace with God it didn't even matter anymore. No longer did I want to hang on the promise but the promiser. God had me at the place that no matter what happened in the end my relationship was secure with Him. You see my friend all God really wants is you to want Him as much as He wants you. He tries to get our attention by us seeking after this great reward hoping that in the end we find the greater reward. I found the greater reward by sitting in the waiting room learning how to wait well. I was seeing the Physician and didn't even know it. Just communing with God and being in his presence was so more valuable than any tangible thing I could hold. I wouldn't trade that for anything in the world. It caused such a discipline in me that it flowed out of me wherever I was at. I had not taken this journey by my own submissiveness but along the way I learned to be submissive to the father and by doing that He surprised me in so many ways by showing me he had my back.

He reminded me that opposition will always come when trying to do and get where He wants you to be. Our goal is to learn how to maneuver through the opposition to get what's waiting for us on the other side. God didn't say it was easy but possible if we would just trust the process.

God encouraged me as I waited and showed me through his word that I am not the only one who had to wait on a promise.

Look at Abraham the father of many nations. God promised to Abraham that he would be the father of many nations. But when the promise was first given Abraham and his wife Sarah did not have any children. God continued, to restate His promise to Abraham through the years. Finally when Abraham was 100 and Sarah was 90 years old God gave them their son Isaac. Though it took years of patiently waiting, they received the promise of God.

Did they mess up at times patiently waiting for the promise, of course they did. But think about the valuable lessons they learned while waiting.

Look at Joseph from pit to prison to palace. A picture of patience while waiting well. Joseph's brothers sold him as a slave. Though he did not understand all that was happening he trusted God to work out His plan in His time. Joseph patiently worked faithfully in each situation he was in. He waited for God to fulfill His promise that Joseph would be a leader of his people. He had to be patience as he believed God, but probably wandered why he was sitting in a prison cell. God did lift Joseph to be a great powerful leader to his people.

Look at Job the man of patience. God allowed the devil to destroy everything Job owned. Job was a wealthy man. He had it all. Job went through a lot and even lost his children. However, Job did not blame God. He accepted that God had a plan and would be patience for God to reveal his plan. Job friends even tried to find out what great sin he had committed but Job knew that sometimes bad things happen to good people. Job knew God had a plan and was willing to accept what God allowed in his life. In the end God restored to Job twice as much as he had in the beginning. How many of us can say we would have been able to endure what Job went through.

God said Look at you. Ta-Tanisha, breaking down barriers. A promise given a long time ago. Stating you would set many woman and men free from bondage with woody ideas and creativity. Breaking the shackles off the people and having them to return back unto God. No matter how great the task and how things were falling apart in my own life. I stayed the course to receive his promise.

If you take a look at these great women and men of God you can see it wasn't easy at all waiting for the promise. They went through much opposition on their journey to get to the promise. It seems as if all their promises were concerning something that God wanted them to do for Him. It had nothing to do with them at all. I truly believe that if you submit to God's purposes and plans for your life it will be well worth the wait.

I hope if you're reading this book it has helped you to learn why it is so important to know how and why to wait well on God. To understand that you should enjoy your journey not be in a hurry to get there. The greatest reward you can ever receive is returning back to the father, even if he has to dangle a carrot in front of your face to get you there.

I will leave you with this prayer:

> Thank you Lord that you cared so much for me that you have gotten this book in my hands. Not just another book to read and to say it was a great story but a book that has caused me to take a look at my life and make some changes. Not to make some changes today and forget about them tomorrow but some changes that are for a lifetime. Father forgive me if I have been stuck in old habits and stinking thinking. Father forgive me if I have been doing things my way instead of your way. Father forgive me if I have put all my trust in self, people and things and have not trusted you. Forgive me if my faith level is not where it is supposed to be and I have caused myself to take roads that I am familiar with instead of following a voice that I can't see. Forgive me if I have been chasing after things instead of chasing after you. Forgive me for I am weak and not strong enough to carry out your plans and purposes for my life. Father I need you because this stuff is temporary but I need something that is everlasting. Take my hand and lead, guide and direct me. Anoint my eyes to see what you are showing me and anoint my ears to hear what you are saying to me and a heart to receive it. Thank you that I am no longer shackled by fear, doubt or unbelief but stepping out with the Holy Spirit leading the way. Thank

you that opposition will no longer run me in the other direction but I will take on the principles that it will teach me. Show me the distractions from afar off so I can bring them to you quickly. Let prayer and meditations be the first thing on my mind and let me long for the relationship as much as you long for it. I give you my ashes so you in return can give me your beauty. Give me the desire to wait well and not abort the mission. I give you me Lord to do what you will. Amen.

I believe that if you said this prayer and meant it God heard you and will answer you. God will do what He promised.

Printed in the United States
By Bookmasters